© Luke Osborne

This book came about after the re... speaking and debating simply doesn't exist in Primary Education. Hopefully this will change, starting with this book.

Luke Osborne
Worthing, Sussex
Instagram: @Worthingdad
Twitter: @MrOzzyMaths

PROLOGUE

Children should be taught public speaking and it should be taught from a young age. The opening pages of this book will identify how public speaking practice will benefit children and highlight the key ideas behind great public speaking.

The book will then lead into 70 debate inducing questions and statements to base your public speaking sessions around. There is often an opinion with teachers, myself included, that there isn't enough time to teach more than is currently on the national curriculum. Finding ways to link debate opportunities into the current curriculum is vital. With this book in mind, you need to consider: *How can I include an opportunity to discuss and debate for 15-30 minutes in my weekly plans?*

Having a collection of considered debate questions ready to go will allow schools to easily teach public speaking and debating in their week. I have included a few key rules to allow for a free flowing, and respectful, debate.

It is vital that children from a young age are encouraged to form their own opinions and make their own judgements. This will not only help with a child's speaking and listening development but will also have a positive influence on their confidence and moral compass; making children positive citizens of the world.

THE ABILITY TO SPEAK

We've all been there, watching professional public speakers, TED talks, comedians and politicians. Often in awe of how they can speak with such power, inspiration and clarity. It is easy to believe that people either can, or can't, when it comes to public speaking.

However, there are many 'easy to implement' techniques which can revolutionise any presentation, speech, talk or sharing of opinions at all. These techniques, when nurtured, allow children to learn an invaluable life skill. Giving children the opportunities to develop public speaking and debating is an essential skill for future life.

The benefits of being a confident public speaker are undeniable. There is no doubt that it sets you up in life, enabling you to communicate effectively which leads to more opportunities across the board. Being able to hold a room can be invaluable as a child starts to move onto high school and where the debating opportunities will no doubt increase. This life skill cannot be underestimated.

There are 70 possible debate questions contained in this book. These pages feature ideas to help promote healthy debate in your classroom. It is vital you don't deliver your own opinion in the sessions. There is no 'best' answer. Linked to each debate question or statement I have outlined briefly some questions and ideas which are intended to help stimulate debate as required. These prompts are not the ultimate guide as each group reacts differently to each debate therefore you must think on your toes as an educator.

A final answer can only come after a healthy debate and only be decided by your group. An agreed consensus will not always come and isn't required for it to be considered a successful debate.

Each statement has a quote linked to it. They have been added for interest and stimulation for the debate. They can be shared with the group as you see fit.

However, don't allow your class to believe that just because someone has a published quote it means they are right! That is the pleasure of the debating, and the more experience your class have with that the more their skill set will increase: leading to improved public speaking confidence as well.

HOW THE SESSIONS CAN WORK

Below I have outlined three different typical sessions, taking you from starting out sessions, to improving and then the final session which includes ideas which are based on the more traditional debating sessions you will recognise.

The first one is centred on open discussion, any child can put their hand up and engage in the discussion at any moment. With the discussion based debate, I suggest choosing topics that are considered 'easier' to begin with. Choose a stimulus that you think your class would be interested in before moving onto the more philosophical debates.

I must reiterate, it is important that you do not at any point share your own opinion. By all means share interesting questions to develop the children's own opinions and judgements but do not take sides at any point. I accept it can be tricky, but it is of the utmost importance that you follow this rule.

Level One Debating Session:

Discussion based

Starter:

Display the motion (question or sentence) on the board.

Main Task:

Ask children to share their initial thoughts on the motion. To begin with you are likely to only have the confident public speakers engage with the initial discussion. After a few minutes of opening thoughts, ask the class to jot down their own opinions about the stimulus. You may wish to also offer a few extra snippets of information to help. Some children may wish to share their thoughts and opinions with a partner or group verbally rather than write it down.

Now you can select children with and without their hands up, every child should have either written something down or heard someone else's opinion in those few minutes.

Plenary:

After the discussion, share what you feel was the underlying arguments for each side and ask the class to vote on their preferred option. Voting is optional - some children may be undecided and that is ok. It is important however to explain after the vote which side you felt had the strongest arguments and why that is.

This is the chance for the children to learn how to improve. I will repeat here again, you must do this without including your own opinions. I will often tell the children that I will be avoiding sharing personal views, so it is clear and obvious to them.

For example you could say, "I enjoyed hearing both sides of the debate and thought there were some excellent examples and arguments supporting your different opinions. As a class you have voted for this side of the argument. I felt Harley's point about adults and children being ultimately the same because we are all humans a very powerful idea. In my opinion I feel the ideas supporting adults and children being the same was the strongest today. However, if we were to have this debate again in a few weeks time the other arguments may have become more convincing."

Although it is important to jump in to stimulate a debate at times, this should only be done when absolutely necessary. Children must be given as much time as possible to learn and develop their confidence.

Level Two Debating Session:

Pop up Pot Debates

These debates are quick and easy to pick up and go without much preparation. This is the best way to bring debate to a session on the spur of the moment.

You literally put a selection of motions (questions) into a pot and get a child to select one at random. Select two speakers at random (or ask for volunteers), one to speak for and one to speak against. With no time to prepare a speech it is great fun and allows the children to think on their feet.

After the speakers have made their points, ask children to put their hands up and contribute any other thoughts, questions and opinions. Follow this with a blind vote to see whether the motion (question) is agreed with or not.

I enjoy keeping track of the debate questions, speakers and vote results across the year. With this information you can ensure the speakers are varied, if there are any patterns and also what questions you have already covered so far.

Level Three Debating Session:

Traditional Session

Starter:

Display stimulus (question or sentence) on the board

Main Task:

Split the class into two teams. Vary how you split the class across the sessions. You must inform the children whether they are arguing for or against the motion.

Being given a side to the debate is useful to force children to think outside of the box, they may be arguing for or against what they believe in. This however can be tricky, especially for primary school children who are still learning the ropes of what a debate is. This is the hardest level of debate.

Step One:

Gather their points. Using post-it notes can be the most effective. Depending on how tricky the debate question is children may need more input from you (described under each question). I suggest allowing children to work in micro-groups. For example, if there are 30 in the class, 15 on each side, and 4 groups of 3-4.

Step Two:

Next they need to pick their best 5-6 points supporting their side of the argument. Recommend they remove their weakest points and bring together any similar points to make them more powerful. In this step they will also need to think about who is going to be the speaker of their micro-group.

Step Three:

The micro-groups need to write a short structure to their speech they are going to present. Children can consider this simple structure for their points using PEP:
Point: Make their point
Evidence: Support their point with proof
Persuasive: Use powerful language

You may wish to include a word mat for persuasive language to support as required. There is a list of persuasive words and phrases that can be used in a debate at the end of the book.

Step Four:

The 3-4 speakers for each side meet together briefly to decide who is going to present their 2-3 minute speeches first. Whilst the children discuss this plan, you could get the children to write any more points on a post-it note or whiteboard that could come in handy during the debate.

Step Five:

Explain that those not speaking will make up the audience who will get to ask questions and share opinions. These children will get to vote on whether the class carry (agree with) or defeat (disagree with) the motion (question/sentence).

Step Six:

Ensuring the children do not use more than 3 minutes, ask the children to begin their speeches one from each side at a time. Save any questions and extra points from the audience until after the speeches are over. Speakers are allowed to add points with their hands up at the same time as the audience. As chairperson, you must maintain consistent rules.

Step Seven:

When the allotted time for your debate is over, ask the audience to vote. I suggest you get the group to shut their eyes when voting. I find this reduces the 'popularity' vote which can often influence in debates at school age.

Variety:

You can allow the children to choose their sides however learning that every issue has multiple sides is an important lesson of debating. You also want to have a fairly balanced debate team for each one, knowing your class or group is useful in this regard.

1.
IS ANYTHING EVER ETERNAL?

Eternity can mean a completely different thing to everyone you speak to. In religious contexts eternity is spoken of many times and often linked to leading a good life. In household contexts it can be linked to love, marriage and friendships.

Is being eternal and being forever the same thing?

Sometimes children will feel they have achieved the answer to this debate in seconds, "Obviously everything can't be eternal," is a common debate ender for some children. It is important children have time to consider their points, with talk partners, before starting any debate.

Yes, things are eternal
Love, memories, history, change…

No, things are not eternal
All things come to an end…

"DEATH LEAVES A HEARTACHE NO ONE CAN HEAL, LOVE LEAVES A MEMORY NO ONE CAN STEAL."

RICHARD PUZ,
AUTHOR

2. CAN USING SOCIAL MEDIA TURN INTO AN ADDICTION?

Social media is how today's world has connected with each other. No wonder we continue to see kids glued to their phones and tablets all the time.

This theme can make use of news articles and statistics to support the addition while balancing it with the benefit of a community that is connected with each other.

Children will often have a lot of opinions on this due to the endless discussions they would have already had with their families about spending too long on their phone scrolling from their multiple social media platforms.

"IN AN OVERWHELMING ATTEMPT TO CAPTURE MEMORIES, PEOPLE HAVE FORGOTTEN TO MAKE MEMORIES."

ABHIJIT NASKAR,
AUTHOR

3.
IS SOME COMMITMENT BETTER THAN OTHERS?

Commitment can mean something completely different from one person to another. Ask the class to share what they consider themselves committed to. Is it school life? Gaming? Sport? Religion? Family?

Why is showing commitment to something a good thing? Can it be a bad thing? Are you able to explain that people often show commitment in a variety of different ways? Can commitment and addiction be considered the same thing?

Yes, some commitment is better than others
Being committed to a sport or religion is better than being committed to gambling or drugs.

No, no commitment is better than others
Commitment and addiction are not the same. Being committed to something shows dedication to a cause or activity that you love. How can we say whether one commitment is more important than another.

"THE WAY YOU DO YOUR WORK IS MORE IMPORTANT THAN HOW MUCH WORK YOU DO."

WESAM FAWZI, ENTREPRENEUR

4.
HOW DO YOU CHOOSE SOMEONE TO DO SOMETHING IMPORTANT?

Life gives us all many opportunities to choose someone to do something important for us. Obviously there are adult roles, special tasks at a wedding, god parents and picking who babysits the children.

However, you want to give the children chance to really delve deep into their lives. Think every day, what is important to them in their lives and who helps them? Why them?

Who did you choose? Why did you choose them? Have you ever been chosen to do something important? Why were you chosen? How did you feel when you were chosen?

"THE IMPORTANT PEOPLE IN OUR LIVES LEAVE IMPRINTS. THEY MAY STAY OR GO IN THE PHYSICAL REAL, BUT THEY ARE ALWAYS THERE IN YOUR HEART, BECAUSE THEY HELPED FORM YOUR HEART. THERE'S NO GETTING OVER THAT."

RACHEL COHN,
WRITER

5.
SHOULD AGREEMENTS, AND PROMISES, BE KEPT?

Children love to keep promises with each other. Often in my year six class I hear, "She **PROMISED** she would keep it secret." Along with, "But we **AGREED** not to tell a teacher."

Why are agreements important? Why should promises be kept? What are the consequences for broken agreements? Who do you have agreements with? How important is it to keep these agreements?

Yes, agreements and promises should be kept
If you don't keep agreements or promises, what is the point of them existing in the first place?

No, not all agreements and promises should be kept
There are obviously sometimes where you cannot keep a promise or agreement. Situations arise where you are no longer able to keep the promise.

"I promised I wouldn't tell anyone, but it was too important to keep secret - I was worried."

**"LIARS MAKE THE BEST PROMISES."
PIERCE BROWN,
SCIENCE FICTION WRITER**

6.
WHAT MAKES AN INFLUENTIAL PERSON?

We are influenced everyday by an incredible amount of people. On TV, social media, YouTube, celebrities, sport stars, pop stars, friends, teachers and family - sometimes people we have met just once and sometimes people we have known a long time.

How have people in your life influenced you? Was it a family member? A friend? A teacher? What did that person do for you that makes you remember them in particular? Is it purely a memory in your mind or are they linked to a hobby, object or situation? Can someone be influential in good and bad ways? Is being an influential person always a positive thing or can it be a negative thing as well?

When discussing negative influences, you may wish to consider your group and their background. Are they likely to 'over-share' information about negative influences? Ensure all children are aware that they do not have to share anything they don't want to.

"SUCCESS ISN'T ABOUT HOW MUCH MONEY YOU MAKE, IT'S ABOUT THE DIFFERENCE YOU MAKE IN PEOPLE'S LIVES."

MICHELLE OBAMA,
ATTORNEY

7.
IF YOU WERE TO CREATE YOUR OWN RELIGION, WHAT WOULD YOU WANT TO BE YOUR TEN COMMANDMENTS?

Religion is a common debating topic, and having a respectful introduction at primary school can have a positive impact on diversity and inclusion. With every child, no matter their religious background, working on their ten commandments can allow children to realise the common beliefs they hold important to themselves match so many others.

For this debate to be successful, children should write their own ten commandments first and then the group can come together and discuss why it is their ten that should make the final list. It is important children realise that even the wording of their commandments has to be scrutinised and debated.

Avoid letting children vote for their favourite commandments at the end, base it on the best arguments. Voting on the results of a debate will usually go the way of the perceived 'most popular', or 'most intelligent', child without any consideration to the debate just had.

"BUT STICKING TO RULES JUST BECAUSE THEY'RE THERE DOES NOT MAKE THEM RIGHT. YOU NEED TO LEARN WHEN THE RULES SHOULD BE BROKEN"

ILSA J. BICK,
AUTHOR

8.
CAN ONE PERSON BELIEVE AN ACTION IS 'GOOD' THAT ANOTHER PERSON BELIEVES IS 'WRONG'?

This can be a very difficult question to discuss and debate. On this page there is multiple scenarios suggested to build upon the debate, to entice children to question, change and expand their own opinions and arguments. Do not use all of the scenarios if you believe they might be a step too far, and don't offer the alternative situation until it has been discussed.

Would you stand up against these people or situations?

A person puts a knife into someone's stomach?

What if that person was a surgeon saving someones life in an operation?

A police officer shoots someone.

What if they were threatening to detonate a bomb in a full shopping centre and it was the only option available to the officer to stop them?

Would your actions change if we thought someone was watching us? Children need to realise that our actions are sometimes dependant on what we think will happen to us if someone sees us do them. Do we make different decisions if we think no-one will know about our actions?

"REAL INTEGRITY IS DOING THE RIGHT THING, KNOWING THAT NOBODY'S GOING TO KNOW WHETHER YOU DID IT OR NOT"

OPRAH WINFREY, TALK SHOW HOST

9.
IS WAR EVER RIGHT?

Avoiding your own opinion on this is usually tricky with this debate topic. Try to keep a lid on children who want to talk about the glorification of war based on their favourite films or computer games. This must be done without dampening the debate however.

How do you feel about war? Is war ever right? Is war ever considered to be a 'good' action? Can you imagine any situation which would make you decide to fight in a war? What are the alternatives?

Yes, war can be right
Without war we would never be able to ensure the people who want to ruin the world and other people's lives were stopped. Think of Hitler, for example.

No, war is never right
If everyone had access to the right support and education in life there wouldn't be war. It were all just human beings on planet earth working together - war wouldn't be needed. Imagine a world without countries and borders. War is never right, diplomacy is far more useful to the lives of the people.

"WAR IS WHAT HAPPENS WHEN LANGUAGE FAILS."

MARGARET ATWOOD, POET

10.
WHAT DOES LEADING A 'GOOD LIFE' LOOK LIKE?

The Good Life. We all know we have things in our lives that we could maybe alter but does the group believe that leading a good life is quantifiable?

How would you know if someone has lived, or is living, a good life? Who do you think leads a good life? Why do you think that person leads a good life?

Children usually see a person whois always well behaved in their eyes as leading a good life, rarely do they discuss the idea that leading a good life can depend completely on your view on life.

Playing the Xbox all day could literally be the good life to one person, but the worst life to another!

"A MAN WHO DARES TO WASTE ONE HOUR OF TIME HAS NOT DISCOVERED THE VALUE OF LIFE."
CHARLES DARWIN,
SCIENTIST

11.
CAN YOU ACTUALLY THINK ABOUT NOTHING?

We've all been there. Trying to get to sleep whilst our brain races in every direction. You share your 'getting to sleep problems' with friends and family, and along with the suggestion of counting sheep the advice is usually along the lines of, 'you are thinking about too much'.

This idea hints that perhaps it is possible to think about nothing.

Does the brain ever stop thinking? When we are thinking about nothing, are we actually thinking about something?

Is it that we are truly thinking about nothing or are we just having unconscious thoughts? How about people that meditate to calm their minds, do they think about nothing? What do you think?

"I LOVE TO TALK ABOUT NOTHING. IT'S THE ONLY THING I KNOW ANYTHING ABOUT."
OSCAR WILDE,
POET

12.
IF YOU HAD A DIFFERENT NAME, WOULD YOU BE A DIFFERENT PERSON?

Does a name influence the kind of life you have? Homer Simpson once changed his name to Max Power, with his new identity came a big change in attitude, he's more assertive and outgoing. Suddenly, he has respect from everyone…but it is short-lived and he soon returns back to his original name.

Do you think if you had a different name people would view you differently? Would you act differently? How would all of your old friends view you? What would your parents think? Would they take to it, be offended by it, or ridicule you for it?

"MAX POWER, HE'S THE MAN WHOSE NAME YOU'D LOVE TO TOUCH, BUT YOU MUSTN'T TOUCH!"
HOMER SIMPSON,
CARTOON CHARACTER

13.
WHERE WOULD BE THE ONE PLACE YOU WOULD GO IF YOU HAD THE CHANCE TO TRAVEL IN TIME?

This will act more as a discussion than a debate. Children will all have different opinions and some children will want to hear a series of other opinions before making their own informed decision.

Children will, of course, only select a period of time they have learnt about in history lessons across their life. However, some children may say they would go back to be with a loved that is no longer here. Or even to a moment in their life where they were their happiest.

"THE JOURNEY OF A THOUSAND MILES BEGINS WITH A SINGLE STEP."
LAO TZU,
PHILOSOPHER

14.
WHAT IS LOVE?

Would the world be a better place if everyone loved each other?

All love.

What different kinds of love are there? Do you love your family the same way you love eating chocolate or playing Roblox? Would loving your enemy as much as you love other things in your life, make them your friend? What would happen if everyone did it? What if everyone made the hardest effort to love their enemy?

Is loving football and loving your family the same thing?

Be wary of marital breakdowns and other family upsets that could come through this discussion. Ensure you tell children to only share their own thoughts and feelings if they feel comfortable with doing so.

"'TIS BETTER TO HAVE LOVED AND LOST, THAN NEVER TO HAVE LOVED AT ALL."
LORD TENNYSON,
POET

15.
IS EVERYTHING CONNECTED?

Thinkers from all ages and cultures have discussed the idea that we are all connected and that everything we do affects everything else. The butterfly effect is a commonly used metaphor.

What do the children think about that?

When you say something horrible to someone, what might happen to them? How could the course of their day or week alter by your actions? Could that create a knock on affect to other people's lives? What could've been different for them if you had been nice or hadn't said anything at all?

Lots of children will want to link this to social media as well.

"WE ARE LIKE ISLANDS IN THE SEA, SEPARATE ON THE SURFACE BUT CONNECTED IN THE DEEP."
WILLIAM JAMES, PSYCHOLOGIST

16.
CAN KINDNESS CHANGE THE WORLD?

If you act well, things will be good. If you don't act well, things will be bad.

Often you hear about how good random acts of kindness are such good thing. People say that if only everyone was kind the world would be a better place.

But is that really the case?

"JUST ONE ACT OF KINDNESS CAN CHANGE SOMEONE'S WHOLE WORLD."
HEATHER WOLF,
AUTHOR

17.
WOULD YOU EAT MEAT, IF THE ANIMAL COULD TALK TO YOU?

We know animals communicate with each other in some way. If you think of dolphins, dogs and chimpanzees as a well-known example.

Imagine you were ordering your fried breakfast with bacon, would you think differently if the pig was able to talk to you?

Just because it doesn't speak does that mean it should be eaten? Is it our responsibility to look after all animals on the planet, not just humans?

Some people will say that eating the right kinds of meat are important to our diet. It is high in protein, B-vitamins and Iron which are all an important part of a healthy diet. Does the idea of animals being able to talk to you put you off eating meat despite being an essential part of many human's daily diet?

"I CHOOSE NOT TO MAKE A GRAVEYARD OF MY BODY FOR THE ROTTING CORPSES OF DEAD ANIMALS."
GEORGE BERNARD SHAW, PLAYWRIGHT

18.
IS THE WORLD TRULY GREAT?

It is hard to always notice things because we are so busy. Staring at multiple screens all day long, spending evenings doing homework or playing computer games - maybe if we spent more time stopping and looking around we might notice the greatness in the world.

Have you ever seen patterns and shapes form in the clouds? Have you ever appreciated the bright colours around you, the colours of food, flowers or the sunset and sunrise?

Have you ever stood on a hill top, or in front of the sea, closed your eyes, breathed and listened? What could tarnish your view on the world being truly great?

Can the world be great without considerations of humans? Or is it impossible to have a great world considering what humans do? War, famine, murder, racism all exist in the human world. Does that mean the world cannot be truly great?

"THE WORLD IS A BOOK AND THOSE WHO DO NOT TRAVEL READ ONLY ONE PAGE."
ST. AUGUSTINE, PHILOSOPHER

19.
CAN YOU THINK YOURSELF HAPPY?

Does focusing on happiness, being in a good mood, thinking positively, actually work? Is it possible to convince yourself you are happy all the time?

How can we make it work? Quite often people will tell others to, 'snap out of it,' and, 'stop being so grumpy.' But is it as easy as that? Sometimes people will just want time alone, time to relax, time to unwind before they will feel happy again.

Some people think that if you think optimistically, positively, creatively and have purposeful and elevated thoughts you can change your mind set no matter how unhappy you are.

Whereas these are definitely strong arguments, even if you could think yourself happy sometimes, could you always think yourself happy?

"FOLKS ARE USUALLY ABOUT AS HAPPY AS THEY MAKE THEIR MINDS UP TO BE."
ABRAHAM LINCOLN,
POLITICAL LEADER

20.
ARE THERE ANY DIFFERENCES BETWEEN ADULTS AND CHILDREN?

Do us adults always get it right? Do children sometimes out smart adults? Do grown ups forget that life is short and sometimes you just need to have fun? What can children learn from adults and adults learn from children?

Obviously, from a legal stand point there are differences between adults and children. Adults can own property, live alone, vote, drink alcohol, go to prison, take on debt, qualify for a career orientated job. Some adults will believe that the older they are the wiser they are - is that always the case?

Biologically children and adults vary in many ways as well - although we are all human beings. Size being an obvious one.

Does a child's mental ability, concentration and social development vary to that of an adult? Does an adult's life experiences alter the differences between them as well?

Does a 95 year old human's life possess the same value as a 3 year olds?

"ADULTS ARE JUST OBSOLETE CHILDREN AND THE HELL WITH THEM."
DR. SEUSS,
AUTHOR

21.
WHAT IS FRIENDSHIP?

Is friendship important? Why do you choose your friends? How do you choose your friends? What makes friends stay around for a long time, and other friends come and go like the wind? Are people who are only friends a short time really friends?

Can you put a limit of friendship? Is it possible to dislike or even despise your friend? Is it possible to be friends with someone completely different to you? By difference, I mean in terms of their beliefs, lifestyle, opinions, hobbies, race etc.

"FRIENDSHIP IS UNNECESSARY, LIKE PHILOSOPHY, LIKE ART... IT HAS NO SURVIVAL VALUE; RATHER IT IS ONE OF THOSE THINGS WHICH GIVE VALUE TO SURVIVAL."
C.S. LEWIS,
AUTHOR

22.
ARE THE BEST THINGS IN LIFE FREE?

Adults often say the phrase, 'the best things in life are free.' Is that right? Are they? Friends, family, memories and moments are all free but things you love may cost money too? What do you love at your home, or where do you love to go, that costs money?

If you pay to go to a cafe and you always remember the time your friend made such a good joke you fell off your chair sending your milkshake flying, is that a free memory? Or is that a memory which actually cost you money?

Getting attention from parents, family and friends is free, would you include that in the 'best things' category?

"THE BEST THINGS IN LIFE AREN'T THINGS."
ART BUCHWALD,
AMERICAN HUMORIST

23.
CAN ONE PERSON CHANGE THE WORLD?

Sometimes it is hard to believe that one person can change the world. Sometimes you can feel like your one action will never be noticed by anyone.

If you were extra careful and made sure your household recycled everything you possibly could, would that change the world? Or would it just be part of a bigger picture, a small contribution in a huge world? Is that the same as changing the world?

Can the class name anyone (or any children) who have changed, or impacted, the world in recent times?

- Greta Thunberg
- Kelvin Doe
- Malala Yousafzai
- Iqbal Masih
- Anne Frank

Have the children heard of any of these people?

What did they do?

"EVERYONE THINKS OF CHANGING THE WORLD, BUT NO ONE THINKS OF CHANGING HIMSELF."
LEO TOLSTOY,
WRITER

24.
IS IT WORSE TO FAIL AT SOMETHING OR NEVER ATTEMPT IT IN THE FIRST PLACE?

Fear of failure is something that puts a lot of people off trying new things. Why is that? Is failure really something that we should to be frightened of?

The fear of failure is very real.

Failure can bring upset, stress and embarrassment. However, most people also accept the idea that failing at something is the best way to learn to be better at that something in the long term.

"EVERYTHING YOU WANT IS ON THE OTHER SIDE OF FEAR."
JACK CANFIELD,
AUTHOR

25.
IS IT POSSIBLE TO BE KIND TO EVERYONE ALL THE TIME?

Is it really possible? People often say the world needs a little more kindness to make it a better place. But how realistic is the notion that we can be kind to everyone all the time?

Some people will point to mood for a point, if you are sad or in a particularly bad mood it is hard to be kind. Is not being kind to someone the same as being mean?

Some people will say being kind is such a simple and small gesture usually that we shouldn't have any trouble always being kind.

Others often point to the idea that some people don't deserve kindness in their life. Do you agree with this?

"THE SIMPLEST OF ACTS OF KINDNESS ARE BY FAR MORE POWERFUL THAN A THOUSAND HEADS BOWING IN PRAYER"
MAHATMA GANDHI,
POLITICAL LEADER

26.
SHOULD EVERYONE GIVE TO CHARITY?

How do we define 'give'? Are we talking about money, time, effort or something else? Or are we talking about all of it?

Should you be guilt tripped into helping someone out because it is for charity? Should you have to give money to a sponsored event just because it is for charity?

Do you believe people with more money should give more money to charity? Is that the right thing to do? Is that fair?

"I HAVE FOUND THAT AMONG ITS OTHER BENEFITS, GIVING LIBERATES THE SOUL OF THE GIVER."
MAYA ANGELOU,
POET

27.
IS HOMEWORK SOMETHING YOU SHOULD HAVE TO DO?

Would never doing any homework have an impact on your life? Are you happier to do homework if it is fun? Can you make all homework fun?

Imagine a time when you don't do homework, have you ever felt guilty about not doing it? What do you think caused the guilt? Was it the worry of an angry teacher or was it because you let yourself down? Did the guilt last forever?

What positive impact could there be on your life by always doing your homework to the best of your ability?

"HOMEWORK IS A TERM THAT MEANS GROWN UP IMPOSED YET SELF-AFFLICTING TORTURE."
JAMES PATTERSON,
AUTHOR

28.
SHOULD YOU BE REWARDED FOR WORKING HARD IN SCHOOL?

What is the reward for your hard work in school? Should schools be awarding you something for your effort? Should you work for your own benefit? What reward would motivate you to work harder in school?

When you leave school, what rewards do you get in life for working hard? We always talk to children about working hard because you want to get better at something or understand more of a subject. Is that what it is like for adults?

If an adult worked hard, and went above and beyond all the time in their job - they would expect a pay rise!

**"EDUCATION IS THE KEY TO UNLOCKING THE WORLD, A PASSPORT TO FREEDOM."
OPRAH WINFREY,
TALK SHOW HOST**

29.
WHAT IS THE LINE BETWEEN ART AND NOT ART?

Is there a line? In your art lessons doesn't your teacher often say, don't worry you can't get it wrong - it is art after all?
How do you distinguish the differences between the idea that something can and cannot be art?

Some would say there isn't a line at all.

There are people who would say anything can be classed as art. If someone decides something is making a statement then that is art. If there is the intention for something to be art, then that is art.

Is something classed as art if it is not appreciated?

Some people will exclaim when looking at certain paintings, 'that is NOT art!'

Why is that?

"EVERY CHILD IS AN ARTIST. THE PROBLEM IS HOW TO REMAIN AN ARTIST ONCE WE GROW UP."
PABLO PICASSO,
ARTIST

30.
DOES FATE EXIST?

A commonly said phrase, 'it was fate.' The idea that it was destiny for something to happen.

"Oh, I knew for sure I was going to get that question wrong, it was fate."

But if fate really does exist, does that mean we are not of free will? Does that mean we don't choose anything we do? If it was already planned out for us, it was surely fate.

Or, is the idea of something being fate just a turn of phrase for something that you felt was likely to happen.

Is it possible for fate to both exist and not exist at the same time?

"DO NOT BE AFRAID; OUR FATE CANNOT BE TAKEN FROM US; IT IS A GIFT"
DANTE ALIGHIERI,
AUTHOR

31.
WHAT MAKES SOMETHING SACRED?

What does the term sacred even mean? What does it mean to you? Sometime we have words we use in our life which carry certain meaning to something. Can we use words steeped in religious connotations to describe every day things in our life? What we do, who we are?

What really makes something scared?

One definition is:

> *'connected with God or dedicated to a religious purpose and so deserving veneration'*

Another is:

> *'regarded with great respect and reverence by a particular religion, group, or individual'*

And finally:

> *'regarded as too valuable to be interfered with.'*

"THE INTUITIVE MIND IS A SACRED GIFT AND THE RATIONAL MIND IS A FAITHFUL SERVANT. WE HAVE CREATED A SOCIETY THAT HONOURS THE SERVANT AND HAS FORGOTTEN THE GIFT."
ALBERT EINSTEIN,
SCIENTIST

32.
IS BELIEVING IN KARMA A GOOD THING?

The idea that if someone was to do something bad to someone karma would come around and balance the universe. It is the idea that the person who did the bad deed would suffer an equally bad deed done onto themselves.

But is that a good way to explain away bad things? Is wishing bad things onto someone else the best way to cope in life?

Picture this: You are tired and stressed. Your best friend is no longer your friend. You are not feeling well either. You lose your temper with someone quite severely and end up saying bad words to them which leaves them very upset.

Is it fair that the person you said it to wished a similar event would now come to you in the near future? Or would you prefer that the person recognises the situation you find yourself in and accepts your apology?

"AN EYE FOR AN EYE WILL MAKE THE WORLD BLIND."
GHANDI,
POLITICAL LEADER

33.
DO FOOTBALLERS EARN TOO MUCH MONEY?

Why do they earn so much money? Most Premier league footballers are on at least £30,000 a week, with the highest paid players earning over £500,000 a week. Shouldn't a doctor or a fire fighter get paid more?

There is no getting away from the fact that footballers earn a lot more than your average salary. But is it footballers fault? Teams want the best players and just like in any business, demand for the best players drive up prices and wages.

Are we also forgetting the sacrifice that these players have made? Loss of time with friends and families pursuing this limited dream?

"IF YOU TAKE THE MONEY AWAY, A LOT OF THE FOOTBALLERS WOULD STILL BE PLAYING FOOTBALL. SO, THE MONEY HAS NOTHING TO DO WITH IT."
ALAN SHEARER,
FOOTBALLER

34.
BOOKS ARE ALWAYS BETTER THAN FILMS

This is a commonly heard phrase when a film has been turned into a book or the other way round. Are books always better than the film? Could this always be the case? What is it about a book?

Thinking about real examples can assist the debate.

Lord of the Rings, Harry Potter or Gone Girl for example.

Films can be enjoyed socially and they are quicker to watch. Books develop your imagination, carry more details than films and can improve your literacy skills.

"BOOKS ARE ALWAYS BETTER THAN MOVIES! THEY ARE READY WHEN YOU ARE. YOU ARE A PARTICIPANT AND NOT A MERE OBSERVER. YOU MAKE THE DECISIONS WHAT THINGS LOOK LIKE, OR OUGHT TO."
JOHN LEONARD,
CRITIC

35.
CAN ANYONE BELONG TO A COMMUNITY?

What does it mean to belong to a community? Do you belong to a community? Are you alone if you do not have that sense of belonging somewhere, a part of something bigger than just yourself?

For communities to work, they need people, for people to feel a part of something they need a community.

What communities do you belong to? Sports club? School? Family? Town? Church?

Is anyone allowed to belong to your communities?

"ONE OF THE MOST IMPORTANT THINGS YOU CAN DO ON THIS EARTH IS TO LET PEOPLE KNOW THEY ARE NOT ALONE."
SHANNON L. ALDER,
AUTHOR

36.
IS IT EVER OK TO LOSE YOUR TEMPER?

This will bring up a whole host of different situations that will impact children's opinions. Some will say it is ok to lose your temper as long as you don't hurt anyone. Others will believe that you should be able to always control your temper.

This debate allows for children to explore emotions they experience and learn how different people are affected by them.

It is important for people to know that it can sometimes be really difficult for people to hold their anger and there can be a point where it just all comes out. However, society does tell us to contain our anger at all times.

The idea of containing anger can have a negative impact on a person's mental health.

"A QUICK TEMPER WILL MAKE A FOOL OF YOU SOON ENOUGH."
BRUCE LEE,
ACTOR

37. CAN SOMETHING LOGICAL EVER NOT MAKE SENSE?

Something may seem logical to you but to some people your logical notion may not make sense. That said, the pure definition of something that is logically valid is that it makes sense.

Can logic vary from person to person? Does what another person do have to make logical sense to you for it to be classed as logical?

Some people may say that logic and sense have been interchanged so much by people that the distinction between the two have been confused.

Can logic change? Is logic and sense two very different things?

"A MIND ALL LOGIC IS LIKE A KNIFE ALL BLADE. IT MAKES THE HAND BLEED THAT USES IT."
RABINDRANATH TAGORE,
POET

38.
WHAT ARE THE BEST THREE PERSONAL ATTRIBUTES A HUMAN SHOULD POSSESS?

This will really vary from person to person. Will they be attributes to get your by socially, in work or in sport? What makes one personal attribute more desirable than another?

Is it worth considering having what is traditionally known as a negative attribute? Can jealousy, for example, be seen as a best attribute?

Get the group to decide on their best three, based on the best arguments.

"YOU POSSESS ALL THE ATTRIBUTES OF A DEMAGOGUE; A SCREECHING, HORRIBLE VOICE, A PERVERSE, CROSS-GRAINED NATURE AND THE LANGUAGE OF THE MARKET-PLACE. IN YOU ALL IS UNITED WHICH IS NEEDFUL FOR GOVERNING."
ARISTOPHANES,
THE KNIGHTS

39.
SHOULD PEOPLE BE REQUIRED TO VOTE BY LAW IN ELECTIONS?

The idea of a democracy is that everyone that is legitimate according to the laws of a democratic nation, gets a chance to have a say on who runs the country.

The idea of compulsory voting is that all legitimate citizens of a country would get a say on who runs the country for the next 4 or 5 years. This would mean 100% of the legitimate population of a country would vote. Usually a far smaller amount of legitimate voters actually vote, especially in smaller, local, elections.

Some people believe voting to be a right to choose to do or not do. They believe it is their human right to not vote if they wish it so. If they don't believe in any of the candidates in an election why should they have to vote for one of them?

"THE BEST ARGUMENT AGAINST DEMOCRACY IS A FIVE-MINUTE CONVERSATION WITH THE AVERAGE VOTER."
WINSTON CHURCHILL,
POLITICAL LEADER

40.
WHEN PEOPLE SUCCEED, IT IS BECAUSE OF HARD WORK AND NOTHING TO DO WITH LUCK

There have been actual studies completed on this which have suggested the most successful people, measured by wealth, have a very large degree of luck along the way. However, it is also pointed out in the study that the harder you work, the more it pays of in the long run.

Some people say that successful people are either lucky or just got to where they are due to knowing the right people to opened the right doors.

Others say working hard allows you to unlock those doors yourself.

"IT'S HARD TO BEAT A PERSON WHO NEVER GIVES UP."
GEORGE 'BABE' RUTH, BASEBALL PLAYER

41.
IS IT BETTER TO GET VERY GOOD AT ONE THING OR TO BE ALRIGHT AT LOTS OF DIFFERENT THINGS?

Being good at anything always warrants a good old pat on the back. However, is it better to concentrate your time on being excellent at one thing or spread yourself around and try to be alright at lots of things?

Some people may say it depends on what you are trying to achieve. Do you want to be a scientist? Then working extra hard at Science is going to help that. But what about if you don't have a future career in mind but want to concentrate on being very good at just one thing. Like a sport?

Which would you rather be?

Very good at one thing or alright at lots of things?

"BELIEVE IN YOURSELF. YOU ARE BRAVER THAN YOU THINK, MORE TALENTED THAN YOU KNOW, AND CAPABLE OF MORE THAN YOU IMAGINE."
ROY T. BENNETT, AUTHOR

42.
CAN WE REPLACE TEACHERS WITH COMPUTERS?

This is quite an interesting topic that would work wonders for kids in school and be quite a riot among the audience, as well. Obviously nothing can replace us real life, in the flesh, teachers, right?

Apart from being a fun topic, replacing teachers with computers is pretty pertinent in this digital age, with advancements in technology, and artificial intelligence reaching new heights. Various themes around digital learning will begin to arise as well, especially with their recent experiences with home learning across various digital platforms to pull upon.

"A TEACHER THAT CAN BE REPLACED BY A MACHINE SHOULD BE."
SUGATA MITRA,
COMPUTER SCIENTIST

43.
IS EXPLORING SPACE REALLY IMPORTANT?

Space exploration has always been a theme to be debated for many years. Even today, kids will have different perspectives on the subject.

We just need to look at all of the problems we suffer currently on Earth, such as climate change and war which needs our time and attention.

On the other hand, some believe that space exploration is the answer to it. Space exploration has been the very reason we have achieved numerous technological advances of today, which could lead to our salvation?

What do students think about the idea of Astronauts planning to travel to Mars? Do they consider an important thing?

"EARTH IS A SMALL TOWN WITH MANY NEIGHBOURHOODS IN A VERY BIG UNIVERSE."
RON GARAN, ASTRONAUT

44.
ARE ZOOS BENEFICIAL TO ANIMALS IN ANY WAY?

An interesting debate topic for kids, this theme would help kids explore their views about the freedom of animals. This will reach a conflict point where conservation of animals versus making them a showpiece for humans to observe will clash with each other.

People should stop going zoos because animals are kept captive and that is unnatural.

People should keep going to zoos because they look after endangered species and help to educate people about what is being done to look after animals across the world.

"THE VOICE OF THE NATURAL WORLD WOULD BE, 'COULD YOU PLEASE GIVE US SPACE AND LEAVE US ALONE TO GET ALONG WITH OUR OWN LIVES AND OUR OWN WAYS, BECAUSE WE ACTUALLY KNOW MUCH BETTER HOW TO DO IT THAN WHEN YOU START INTERFERING."
JANE GOODALL, ANTHROPOLOGIST

45.
DOES THERE NEED TO BE A CHANGE IN THE AGE FOR VOTING?

With the digital penetration reaching a significant point today, there is a massive shift in the age when people begin to become more aware of their country and its politics.

While one side might argue that reducing the age will allow more youth to choose the leaders they want, others might say that the current age is appropriate, as voting calls for maturity.

"I AM NOT SURE THAT WE WOULD ALWAYS WANT 16-YEAR-OLDS TO DO ALL THE THINGS THEY CAN DO. I AM AFRAID THAT I DO NOT AGREE WITH THE HON. GENTLEMAN ON THE VOTING AGE. I THINK THAT IT SHOULD REMAIN AS IT IS"
TONY BLAIR,
POLITICAL LEADER

46.
SHOULD THE SCHOOL HOURS SHIFT TO BE LATER IN THE DAY?

This is yet another topic that is loved by children and can be quite the favourite for an initial debate. There are a lot of perspectives to covered in this theme, where the focus would shift from the students to the staff of the school as well.

The lifestyles of children and adults come to a clash, creating a peak conflict point. However, quite often children will only think of themselves and their lifestyles in this debate forgetting both sides.

Allocating half the group to argue against this debate is an important option to consider.

"I HAVE NEVER LET MY SCHOOLING INTERFERE WITH MY EDUCATION."
MARK TWAIN,
WRITER

47.
IF A CHILD MAKES A MISTAKE, SHOULD THE PARENTS BE PUNISHED FOR IT?

This theme can quickly get complicated, and children may have difficulty coming to terms with it. There are instances where a child's mistake ends up in a penalty that has to be suffered by the parents.

Some will consider that since children are a result of the upbringing provided by the parents, the argument can be turned to face the other side as well.

This is a very tricky debate question and you should consider the maturity of your class before using this question.

You may also wish to link this debate with the question about how are adults and children different.

"IT'S AMAZING HOW PEOPLE CAN CHANGE BEHIND CLOSED DOORS."
SUSAN FORWARD,
AUTHOR

48.
SHOULD YOU BE MADE TO SAVE YOUR POCKET MONEY OR SHOULD YOU HAVE COMPLETE FREEDOM?

Pocket money is what allows children to explore other facets of life in their early age. While parents tend to provide everything for them, the core point of the allowance is to teach the child a habit of saving and understanding the economy better.

However, children may prefer to look at the allowance as a gift and spent it in ways of their choosing. This will have obvious immediate positives but considering the negatives of not saving any money of time is important.

"A SIMPLE FACT THAT IS HARD TO LEARN IS THAT THE TIME TO SAVE MONEY IS WHEN YOU HAVE SOME."
JOE MOORE,
SINGER-SONGWRITER

49. SHOULD CHILDREN BE ALLOWED PRIVACY IN THEIR LIVES?

Year 6 and 7 especially loves this debate. This is the age they really start to desire, and understand, independence.

11 and 12 year olds are still young and vulnerable in the wider world and parents need to be aware of their activities in order to guide and advise them.

Can a child be trusted to make safe decisions if left unchecked by parents?

Children may wish to discuss parental access to text messages, voice mails and other online chat platforms.

"ALL HUMAN BEINGS HAVE THREE LIVES: PUBLIC, PRIVATE, AND SECRET."
GABRIEL GARCIA MÁRQUEZ,
WRITER

50.
SHOULD YOU SAY 'THANK YOU' TO A ROBOT WAITER?

We teach children to be polite, but for whose sake? Is being polite something you do to make yourself feel accepted in society, or is it something that we should do for the benefit of the person - or thing - we are being polite to?

This topic also throws up the notion of robot consciousness and rights, especially in a world where we've just seen the first robot gain national citizenship in Saudi Arabia

"WHETHER WE ARE BASED ON CARBON OR ON SILICON MAKES NO FUNDAMENTAL DIFFERENCE; WE SHOULD EACH BE TREATED WITH APPROPRIATE RESPECT."
ARTHUR C. CLARKE,
FUTURIST

51.
CAN ANYTHING BE A TOY?

The connection between toys and children runs deep, but these days we can end up thinking that a toy is something that is made by someone else, and made to be a toy.

Children love discussing toy questions, and this one raises issues around ownership as well as purpose and design and the nature of play.

Follow-up questions for those who answer 'yes' might include: 'Can air be a toy?' or 'Can another human be a toy?'

Ultimately, how a child sees the world will influence their opinion here.

"THE COOLEST TOYS DON'T HAVE TO BE BOUGHT; THEY CAN BE BUILT. IN FACT, SOMETIMES THE ONLY WAY THEY'LL EVER EXIST IS IF YOU MAKE THEM YOURSELF."
ADAM SAVAGE,
SPECIAL EFFECTS DESIGNER

52.
CAN A PREGNANT WOMEN EVER BE ALONE?

The ideas of consciousness, what it is to be human and what it is to be alive can be discussed here. A topic for older children, this might trigger other controversial issues to do with women's rights.

Important issues can be explored in a non-moralistic and safe way.

> "THE WOMB IS ONE OF THE FINAL STOPS ON ETERNITY'S JOURNEY."
> MATSHONA DHLIWAYO, ENTREPRENEUR

52.
IS BEING SCARED OF NOTHING WORSE THAN BEING SCARED OF EVERYTHING?

The concept of bravery can be almost stereotypical with children; boys are brave and they protect girls.

TV and books are full of this view, but maybe the 'scared girl' is doing the right things, and the 'big brave male' is making things worse.

Is being scared a good or a bad thing in the first place?

"DON'T BE AFRAID OF BEING SCARED. TO BE AFRAID IS A SIGN OF COMMON SENSE. ONLY COMPLETE IDIOTS ARE NOT AFRAID OF ANYTHING."
CARLOS RUIS ZAFÓN,
AUTHOR

53.
CAN A BLIND PERSON BE RACIST?

It's said that children don't see colour, so is it the sight of difference that provokes feelings of distrust and dislike?

Is racism something that is inherent, or is it taught, and if so, by whom and why?

Can you be accidentally racist, and if so, should job interviews and political debates be held 'blind', rather like the judging system they use in BBC talent show, 'The Voice,' so we are not influenced by skin colour?

"RACE IS SUCH AN INGRAINED SOCIAL CONSTRUCT THAT EVEN BLIND PEOPLE CAN 'SEE' IT. TO PRETEND IT DOESN'T EXIST TO YOU ERASES THE EXPERIENCES OF BLACK PEOPLE."
ZACH STAFFORD,
JOURNALIST

54.
VIDEO GAMES ARE BAD FOR CHILDREN

Most children have had the conversation with their parents about how too much time spent on video games is bad for children.

Evidence does suggest that too much screen time isn't good for your eyes, brain functionality and disrupts sleep.

However, some people see video gaming as a potentially lucrative job nowadays, a social hobby and a chance for them to expand their creativity.

Do the positives outweigh the negatives? Are video games inherently bad for children?

"OVER THE CENTURIES, MANKIND HAS TRIED MANY WAYS OF COMBATING THE FORCES OF EVIL. PRAYER, FASTING, GOOD WORKS AND SO ON. UP UNTIL DOOM, NO ONE SEEMED TO HAVE THOUGHT ABOUT THE DOUBLE BARREL SHOTGUN. EAT LEADEN DEATH, DEMON..."
TERRY PRATCHETT,
AUTHOR

55.
SHOULD SMOKING BE BANNED ENTIRELY?

Smoking is often a contentious discussion. Most often children will support the idea that smoking is very bad for your body and therefore you shouldn't do it.

However adults are free to choose if they wish to take the risk of smoking or not. Should we remove the opportunity for adults to choose to smoke?

Driving a car over 100mph has been banned for your own safety, so why shouldn't smoking be banned too for the same reasons?

"SHE BLEW MORE SMOKE TOWARD ME, A LAZY GAME OF CANCER CATCH."
GILLIAN FLYNN,
AUTHOR

56.
SHOULD ALL PAPER AND NOTEBOOKS BE REPLACED BY DIGITAL DEVICES?

As human beings, we already spend a lot of life staring at a screen. If we replaced all paper and notebooks for a digital device would we lose touch with 'real life'? Is losing the art to write by hand important?

On the other hand, if we did replace all paper and notebooks with digital devices we would have less waste paper which would save trees.

What do you think?

"IF YOU ARE ON SOCIAL MEDIA, AND YOU ARE NOT LEARNING, NOT LAUGHING, NOT BEING INSPIRED OR NOT NETWORKING, THEN YOU ARE USING IT WRONG."
GERMANY KENT,
JOURNALIST

57. TESTS AND EXAMS SHOULD BE ABOLISHED

The benefit of exams and tests has been a hot topic for a long time. Some people see exams as a vital chance to prove you have learnt and understood the material you are being tested on. To these people, being able to 'show off' their acquired knowledge in the form of a test is a fundamental part of education and gaining qualifications.

The other side of the argument looks at whether we should test at all. Stating that getting people to take a one off test after, often, years of learning isn't the most effective way of proving knowledge. They believe that completing an evidence based portfolio is a more beneficial way of proving knowledge and competence for a qualification.

"SCHOOL EXAMS ARE MEMORY TESTS, IN THE REAL-WORLD NO ONE IS GOING TO STOP YOU FROM REFERRING TO A BOOK TO SOLVE A PROBLEM."
AMIT KALANTRI,
AUTHOR

58.
IS IT ALRIGHT TO CHEAT IN A TEST?

Cheating is always a good one for debating. Often children will believe that whether or not they should cheat on a test depends on the importance of the test.

What is the point of a test? Is is alright to cheat in a test? How about if your friend has studied harder than anyone else in the class, but someone who cheated on the exam outscores her? Is that fair?

This debate will address morality implicitly as well.

"DURING A TEST; PEOPLE LOOK UP FOR INSPIRATION DOWN IN DESPERATION, AND LEFT AND RIGHT FOR INFORMATION."
ANONYMOUS

59.
ARE FOOTBALLERS POSITIVE ROLE MODELS FOR CHILDREN?

Who is classed a role model varies depending on a whole host of influences in children's lives. Big supporters of football will often see footballers as positive role models and will cite reasons such as being fit and competing in an elite team sport.

Other children may highlight that as when footballers dive, cheat and argue with the referee, often in an angry fashion this prevents them from possibly ever being positive role models for children. These children may believe that footballers are not good role models for them as they can't control their tempers some times.

This could allow for an extended debate on whether it is ok to be angry and lose your temper, which links nicely to another question in the book.

"CHILDREN HAVE NEVER BEEN VERY GOOD AT LISTENING TO THEIR ELDERS, BUT THEY HAVE NEVER FAILED TO IMITATE THEM."
JAMES BALDWIN,
WRITER

60.
IS IT EVER OK TO STEAL?

Can the children name three occasions when they think it is ok to steal?

Some people believe that there can be a necessity to stealing, such as for the preservation of life, as long as it isn't at odds with the end of another person's life.

Is it ok to steal when you are stealing back something that was stolen from you? Is that ok?

In most Western nations, our museums are filled with stolen artefacts of importance from around the world. Is a country keeping stolen items from another country ok? Is it the same as stealing from the corner shop?

"THE ROBB'D THAT SMILES, STEALS SOMETHING FROM THE THIEF; HE ROBS HIMSELF THAT SPENDS A BOOTLESS GRIEF."
WILLIAM SHAKESPEARE, OTHELLO

61.
WHAT DOES IT MEAN TO RESPECT SOMEONE?

Does respect come from the fear of a person or thing, or does respect come from something else? Are their different ways you could gain respect from someone else?

Are some of these ways better or worse? Is being respectful towards someone because you believe them to be a great role model the same as respecting someone out of fear of what they might do, if you don't respect them?

Who is it that you respect in your life? Why do you respect them? What makes that person respectable?

"IF YOU TRULY WANT TO BE RESPECTED BY PEOPLE YOU LOVE, YOU MUST PROVE TO THEM THAT YOU CAN SURVIVE WITHOUT THEM."
MICHAEL BASSEY JOHNSON, AUTHOR

62.
WOULD YOU RATHER BE THE 99% OR THE 1%?

A well known phrase 'it is always greener on the other side,' comes to mind here. It is often said that 1% of people control 99% of the world's wealth.

Would you rather be in the top 1% wealthiest people in the world, or the other 99% of people?

It seems like an obviously one sided debate, especially when we are talking about using this debate in a classroom. However, forcing one half of the class to argue the benefits of staying in the 'other 99%' group can often spring up a surprising result.

"DON'T GAIN THE WORLD AND LOSE YOUR SOUL, WISDOM IS BETTER THAN SILVER OR GOLD."
BOB MARLEY,
MUSICIAN

63.
WHAT WOULD YOU DO IF YOU HAD 7 DAYS TO CREATE A NEW WORLD?

Imagine you have just been awarded status as a God. You have all the powers you could imagine and are charged with creating a new world.

What does your new world look like? Can you agree with others in your group about certain parts of it? Who would you let live there?

Once you have shared all of your ideas, pose this secondary question:

Would you hang around and stay involved in the world or would you leave it to its own devices?

"A BLANK PIECE OF PAPER IS GOD'S WAY OF TELLING US HOW HARD IT IS TO BE GOD."
SIDNEY SHELDON,
WRITER

64.
DO HEROES EXIST?

Heroes come in various guises. They are often discussed in the news, with friends or on TV programmes and films.

Do they really exist? Do too many people get labelled as a Hero? Does it really matter?

In our society we all love to make a hero out of someone. We have an almost obsession with a belief in a hero.

As an extension on this debate, ask the group to agree on up to ten traits that should be met for someone to be classed as a 'Hero'.

"HEROES ARE MADE BY THE PATHS THEY CHOOSE, NOT THE POWERS THEY ARE GRACED WITH."
BRODI ASHTON,
AUTHOR

65.
IMAGINE YOU OWN A REMOTE CONTROL FOR YOUR LIFE...WHAT WOULD YOU DO WITH IT?

Think of the functions of a remote control. Pause, fast forward, rewind, record…what would you use it for? Would it end up being a curse? What about if you couldn't ever rewind?

Is there particular moments in your life that you would want to go back to? Or moments in your future where you would want to go take a sneak peak at what was to come? Would that tempt you?

Would you ever fast forward if you could never rewind?

"LIFE DOESN'T COME WITH A REWIND, FAST FORWARD OR PAUSE BUTTON. ONCE IT STARTS IT PLAYS UNTIL IT ENDS OR UNTIL YOU PRESS STOP."
SONYA PARKER,
AUTHOR

66.
IF YOU COULD SAVE TEN MILLION PEOPLE BY DYING, WOULD YOU?

Would you do it? Why would you? Why wouldn't you? Would you do it for 1 million other living souls? Ten thousand more people? Would you do it for just two people?

Would it matter who the people were to you? Would it matter if the people you were saving were good or bad people? What if they were criminals? What if they were children? What if they were elderly?

What is right for one person will most certainly be wrong from someone else's perspective.

"SOMETIMES WHEN YOU SACRIFICE SOMETHING PRECIOUS, YOU'RE NOT REALLY LOSING IT. YOU'RE JUST PASSING IT ON TO SOMEONE ELSE."
MITCH ALBOM,
PHILANTHROPIST

67.
WOULD YOU RATHER BE A WELL TREATED SLAVE, OR FREE BUT STRUGGLING TO BARELY SURVIVE?

Why would you choose either option? This debate will obviously bring up slavery and people will have varying opinions to share on this. Is there a perfect answer?

Some people may question whether any of us are truly free or not. Some will say being a well treated slave is the best option because you don't need to worry about survival.

Others will say that without freedom could you have a family? Could you choose to go to the beach? For a country walk? You may barely survive but at least you can make your own choices.

At the end of the debate, get the group to anonymously vote on which they would prefer.

"SOMETIMES EVEN TO LIVE IS AN ACT OF COURAGE."
LUCIUS ANNAEUS SENECA, DRAMATIST

68.
IF IT WERE SCIENTIFICALLY POSSIBLE, WOULD YOU WANT TO LIVE FOREVER?

Imagine scientists have perfected the required processes to allow you to live forever. Is this something you would want to happen to you?

Most people will say that they don't want to die, stating that death is one of the worst parts of living. Lots will suggest they will do anything to prevent death. But if it was possible to live forever and not age nor get frail: would that mean its tempting?

It might be that some people will struggle to explain why, but that they wouldn't want to live forever. Some may state it is linked to the idea that what if their loved ones didn't live forever with them. Others may say that they may simply get bored of life in the end!

**"YOU NEED TO BE GREEDY OR IGNORANT TO TRULY WANT TO LIVE FOREVER."
MOKOKOMA MOKHONOANA, AUTHOR**

69.
IS IT GOOD THAT SO MANY PEOPLE GET ANGRY ABOUT POLITICS THESE DAYS?

This can be easy for some groups to get heavily into a debate whereas some groups can struggle. This debate depends on the family that the children live with. Some will talk more prominently about politics at home whereas some will not. It would be worth asking the children about particular issues and whether they felt their parents got annoyed about them and why that might be.

Contentious issues could involve:
Brexit, Benefit system or immigration

There may be a better option for your group, thinking about particular local issues. Is it good that people are so passionate about certain topics that they can get angry? Or does the group think that it shows people who are so passionate about their political views they are no longer able to listen to all sides of an argument?

"POLITICS IS THE ART OF LOOKING FOR TROUBLE, FINDING IT WHETHER IT EXISTS OR NOT, DIAGNOSING IT INCORRECTLY, AND APPLYING THE WRONG REMEDY."
ERNEST BENN,
PUBLISHER

70.
IS IT EVER RIGHT TO LIE?

Lying is never good. Right? What was the last lie you've told? Who did you tell it to? Was it a BIG lie? Or just a small one? How would you feel if a friend lied to you?

Should you ever tell a lie?

What is a lie? Can anyone define what a lie is? Is it always important to not tell a lie?

Telling a lie will obviously lead to mistrust and can ruin your reputation in a number of ways. But what if you are lying to protect someone, could you still lose the trust of others?

"I'M NOT UPSET THAT YOU LIED TO ME, I'M UPSET THAT FROM NOW ON I CAN'T BELIEVE YOU."
FRIEDRICH NIETZSCHE,
PHILOSOPHER

DEBATE WORDS AND PHRASES

Introductions:
I feel that…
I am sure that…
I think…
For this reason…
On the other hand…
In this situation…

Making your point:
Firstly, Secondly, Thirdly…
Furthermore…
Finally…
Moreover…
Certainly…
Specifically…
Besides…
Likewise…

Details:
For example…
In fact…
For instance…
As evidence…

Ending:
For these reasons…
In short…
Undoubtedly…
Without a doubt…

General sentence starters:
Most people would agree that…
Only a fool would think that…
A sensible idea would be to…
We *all* know that…
Doesn't everyone know that…?
It wouldn't be very difficult to…
The *real* truth is that…
Are we expected to…
Naturally I feel that…
The fact is that…
Everybody knows that…
Surely you would agree that…
Here are two reasons why…
This clearly shows that…
We can see from the evidence that…

ABOUT THE AUTHOR

Luke is a Primary School teacher who works for Sparkle Multi-Academy Trust. He gained his BA (hons) in Learning and Development at Brighton University and completed QTS at Chichester University via the Schools Direct route. In his current role, as a year 6 teacher, he is also RE co-ordinator.

In life outside of work, he is married and the father of two children. He enjoys spending time at the beach, running and singing.

He also co-wrote a short book "The things they didn't teach you at Uni: A guide to being an NQT." with Jamie Parkinson.